OUR FAMILY TREE

· A GENERATIONAL HISTORY ·

INTRODUCTION BY

SHARON LESLIE MORGAN

AUTHOR OF *FINDING YOUR FAMILY TREE*

wellfleet
press

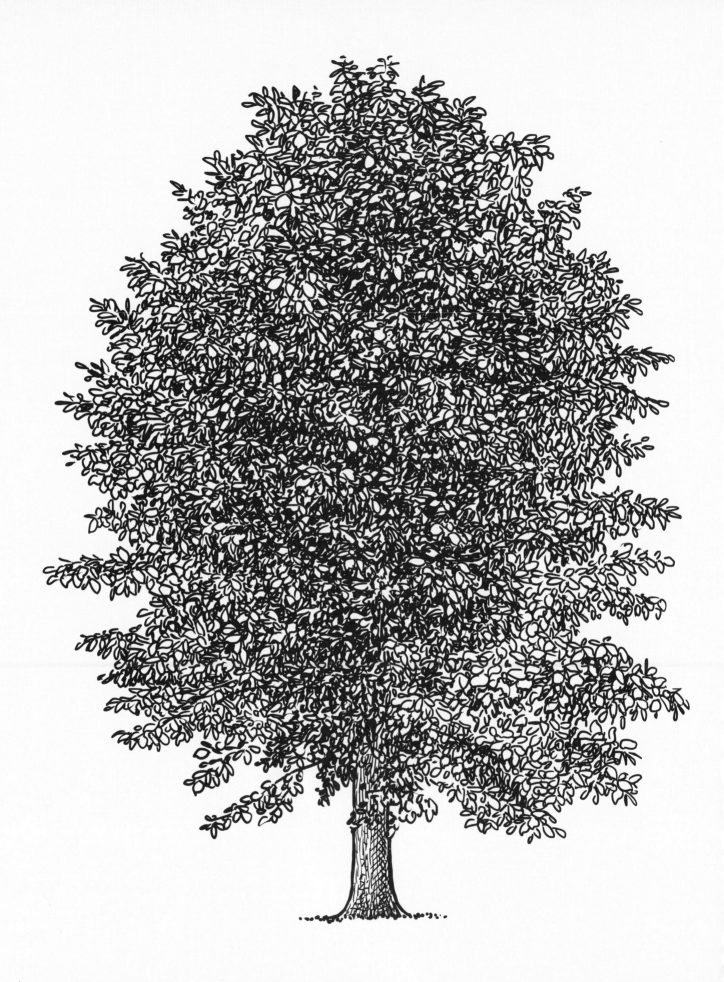

THIS RECORD CONTAINS THE
FAMILY HISTORY AS I KNOW IT OF THE

.... FAMILY

OF .... (PLACE)

COMPILED BY ....

SIGNATURE ....

START DATE ....

Introduction

This record chronicles your personal quest to build and
document your family tree in an inclusive manner.
Each section includes instructions for how to compile
and present your discoveries.

Genealogy is a record of your ancestors:
who they were, when they were born,
where they lived, whom they married, and
who their children were. But the word "family"
doesn't necessarily mean that you are genetically
or genealogically related, or that you have a
traditional family structure.

This record invites you to expand the traditional
genealogy record to include those in your family
who are chosen. You can record this information
on charts that show where everybody fits into your
family schematic.

You will be amazed how quickly your information
adds up. Each generation is approximately twenty-
five years apart, so over the course of one hundred
years, that's four generations. Afterward, numbers
grow exponentially; you plus your parents equals
three, plus their parents equals seven, plus their
parents equals twenty-one. And that doesn't include
all the other relatives: brothers, sisters, aunts,
uncles, nieces, nephews, cousins, and all others of
significance in your life.

Your tree will continue to grow as long as you
continue to research. You can go back as many
generations as you want, knowing that the deeper
you go into the past, the more difficult it will be.

In this process, you must be disciplined about
verifying every bit of information you find. You will
need to locate documents that prove your findings,
and you must keep track of your sources.

Genealogy is as old as recorded time. The word
itself was coined in the fourteenth century. Its

root word is *genealogia*, which means "line of
descent." In every society, people kept track of
community and personal lineages. Long before
the written word, genealogies were preserved
orally. In West Africa, oral historians known
as *griots* memorized tribal history and could
repeat generations of names and community
events out loud, on command. The same concept
of oral tradition springs from India, China, and
many other ancient nations. In Europe, nobles
documented heritage to ensure the inheritance
of crowns and other royal positions. In America, a
land predominantly of immigrants, people arrived
with the stories of their ancestors from far-flung
countries and then made new stories as they
propagated in their adopted homeland.

A good genealogist is also an historian. A
family tree brings your ancestors to life in your
imagination within the context of the times in
which they lived. Bear in mind that the world has
achieved more material and social progress in the
last century than in the preceding millennium.
In the past, most people lived in rural locations,
derived income from agriculture, and were often
poor. Imagine living in a house with no heat other
than a fireplace, no running water, and no indoor
toilet facilities—not to mention no televisions
or smartphones!

Whatever stories you find about your
ancestors—sad, painful, or joyful—your job is
to write things down and preserve them for
posterity. In the end, you'll get a fuller picture of

them and thus a clearer picture of yourself and your family history.

Along the way, you will likely encounter what genealogists call "brick walls." These are seemingly insurmountable barriers to getting the information you need. Don't be discouraged; there are times when you will never find what you are looking for. But then there are times when you will be handsomely rewarded for your attempt to climb over the barriers.

Once you have completed your tree and this journal, pass it along to relatives living now so they can pass it on to those who will be living in the future.

RESEARCH GUIDE

Effective family research entails commitment. It is a long-term journey with many twists and turns. If you are to succeed, you need a road map. That map begins with you, expands to those you know, and then to ancestors in your distant past.

Who do you know that should be in your family tree? Of course, you know yourself, so the very first thing you must do is write down what you know about *you*. When and where were you born? Where did you go to school? Who is your significant other? Do you have children? Grandchildren?

You likely know the people who raised you. But you know them as adults. What about their past? Where did they grow up? Where did they attend school? Did they serve in the military? Were there interesting things about their personalities that made an impact on you?

Do you know your grandparents? What about their parents, your great-grandparents?

As you write your notes, key information that *must* be included for each relative is their name and the dates of their birth, marriages or partnerships, and death, as well as the locations of these events.

You should collect important documents to preserve in your family tree file: birth certificates, commitment or marriage certificates, school documents, Social Security cards, and death certificates. These documents prove identity and are things that future researchers will want to have access to when you are gone. Make it easy for them; include photographs such as baby pictures, birthday parties, graduations, wedding days, and any significant or life-changing events.

A huge resource for tracking your family history is the US census. These exist online, from the very first one in 1790 to the most recently released census in 1950 (due to a seventy-two-year restriction on access to the census).

It is extremely important to keep research notes. You may find something exciting and forget to document where you found it. Don't do that. *Always* write down what you found and where you found it so you can go back to it later, if need be.

Use Family Tree Software

The first tool you need to build your family tree is software. Once you accumulate and organize your notes, the next thing to do is enter it all in one place. Family tree software enables you to do that. You can find what you need almost instantly, connect automatically with online data sources, and create easy-to-read reports. RootsMagic is the recommended software.

Subscribe to Online Data Services

After entering information into your software, the next step is to use online data sources to fill in the blanks and obtain proof documents. The most robust and popular online data sources are Ancestry.com (subscription required) and

> ## THE PROCESS OF FAMILY RESEARCH
>
> • Start with yourself and work backward in time
>
> • Record what you know
>
> • Prove what you can with documentation
>
> • Document all sources
>
> • Save and share your tree and this book with family members

FamilySearch.org (free, although registration is required).

Get Your Family Involved

Genealogical research can be expensive. There are costs associated with subscriptions to online data services and obtaining original documents like birth, marriage, and death records. By getting other family members involved, you may be able to get help paying for some of what you need to be successful. Some of this cost can be abated by asking other family members what documents they have. This is an opportunity for the entire family to share in the joy of discovery.

Sharon Leslie Morgan is a writer, genealogist, and founder of Our Black Ancestry, a website and Facebook group devoted to African American lineage, and the author of Finding Your Family Tree *and* Gather at the Table, *the latter of which won the Phillis Wheatley Award for best nonfiction/memoir at the Harlem Book Fair.*

Research Checklist

Use this checklist to gather the vital information of each
person you research for your family tree.

Vital Records

- ◯ Birth
- ◯ Marriage/Partnership
- ◯ Death

US Census Records

- ◯ 1790
- ◯ 1800
- ◯ 1810
- ◯ 1820
- ◯ 1830
- ◯ 1840
- ◯ 1850
- ◯ 1860
- ◯ 1870
- ◯ 1880
- ◯ 1890
- ◯ 1900
- ◯ 1910
- ◯ 1920
- ◯ 1930
- ◯ 1940
- ◯ 1950

Birth Records

- ◯ Birth Certificate

Death Records

- ◯ Death Certificate
- ◯ Funeral Home
- ◯ Funeral Program
- ◯ Final Place of Rest
- ◯ Grave Marker

Marriage Records

- ◯ Marriage/Commitment Certificate
- ◯ Marriage License
- ◯ Announcement
- ◯ Divorce Petition
- ◯ Divorce Decree

Military Records

- ◯ Draft Card
- ◯ Enlistment Card
- ◯ Pension Applications

Probate Records

- ◯ Will/Administration
- ◯ Property Inventory
- ◯ Estate Settlement

Land Records

- ◯ Deeds
- ◯ Plat Maps/County Maps
- ◯ Land Patents/ Land Grants

Legal Records

- ◯ City Directories
- ◯ Voting Records
- ◯ Tax Lists
- ◯ Court Records
- ◯ Criminal Records

Social Security Records

- ◯ Social Security Number
- ◯ Social Security Death Index

Immigration Records

- ◯ Passenger Lists
- ◯ Naturalization Records

Other

- ◯ State/County
- ◯ Agriculture
- ◯ Mortality

Our Family

This certifies that

....

and

....

were committed to each other on

Month	Day	Year

....

Place of Ceremony

....

....

Ceremony Performed by

....

....

My Genealogy

Full Name

....

....

Birth Date

....

Birthplace

....

Parents' Full Names

....

....

Siblings

....

....

....

....

....

....

....

My Partner's Genealogy

Full Name

....

....

Birth Date

....

Birthplace

....

Parents' Full Names

....

....

Siblings

....

....

....

....

....

....

Our Children

Name	Place of Birth	Date of Birth

Our Grandchildren & Descendants

Name	Place of Birth	Date of Birth

Our Family Tree

My Parent's Full Name
....

My Parent's Full Name
....

Date & Place of Commitment
....

Children
....

....

My Full Name
....

My Partner's Full Name
....

Date & Place of Commitment
....

Our Children
....

....

....

My Partner's Parent's Full Name
....

My Partner's Parent's Full Name
....

Date & Place of Commitment
....

Children
....

....

My Grandparent's Full Name

My Grandparent's Full Name

Date & Place of Commitment

Children

My Grandparent's Full Name

My Grandparent's Full Name

Date & Place of Commitment

Children

My Partner's Grandparent's Full Name

My Partner's Grandparent's Full Name

Date & Place of Commitment

Children

My Partner's Grandparent's Full Name

My Partner's Grandparent's Full Name

Date & Place of Commitment

Children

My Great-Grandparents

Full Name

Full Name

Full Name

Full Name

Full Name

Full Name

Full Name

Full Name

My Great-Great-Grandparents

Full Name

Full Name

Full Name

Full Name

Full Name

Full Name

Full Name

Full Name

Full Name

Full Name

Full Name

Full Name

Full Name

Full Name

Full Name

Full Name

My Partner's Great-Grandparents

Full Name

Full Name

Full Name

Full Name

Full Name

Full Name

Full Name

Full Name

My Partner's Great-Great-Grandparents

Full Name

Full Name

Full Name

Full Name

Full Name

Full Name

Full Name

Full Name

Full Name

Full Name

Full Name

Full Name

Full Name

Full Name

Full Name

Full Name

My Great-Great-Great-Grandparents

Full Name

Full Name

Full Name

Full Name

Full Name

Full Name

Full Name

Full Name

Full Name

Full Name

Full Name

Full Name

Full Name

Full Name

Full Name

Full Name

Full Name

Full Name

Full Name

Full Name

Full Name

Full Name

Full Name

Full Name

Full Name

Full Name

Full Name

Full Name

Full Name

Full Name

Full Name

Full Name

My Partner's Great-Great-Great-Grandparents

Full Name

Full Name

Full Name

Full Name

Full Name

Full Name

Full Name

Full Name

Full Name

Full Name

Full Name

Full Name

Full Name

Full Name

Full Name

Full Name

Full Name

Full Name

Full Name

Full Name

Full Name

Full Name

Full Name

Full Name

Full Name

Full Name

Full Name

Full Name

Full Name

Full Name

Full Name

Full Name

My Ancestral Chart

My Parent's Full Name
....

Date & Place of Birth
....

Date & Place of Commitment
....

Date of Death
....

Place of Burial
....

Occupation(s)
....

....

....

Their Favorite Things
....

....

My Full Name
....

Date & Place of Birth
....

Date & Place of Commitment
....

Date of Death
....

Place of Burial
....

Occupation(s)
....

....

....

My Favorite Things
....

....

....

My Parent's Full Name
....

Date & Place of Birth
....

Date & Place of Commitment
....

Date of Death
....

Place of Burial
....

Occupation(s)
....

....

....

Their Favorite Things
....

....

My Grandparent's Full Name ....

Date & Place of Birth ....

Date & Place of Commitment ....

Date of Death ....

Place of Burial ....

Occupation(s) ....

....

My Grandparent's Full Name ....

Date & Place of Birth ....

Date & Place of Commitment ....

Date of Death ....

Place of Burial ....

Occupation(s) ....

....

My Grandparent's Full Name ....

Date & Place of Birth ....

Date & Place of Commitment ....

Date of Death ....

Place of Burial ....

Occupation(s) ....

....

My Grandparent's Full Name ....

Date & Place of Birth ....

Date & Place of Commitment ....

Date of Death ....

Place of Burial ....

Occupation(s) ....

....

My Great-Grandparents

Full Name
....

Date & Place of Birth
....

Date & Place of Death

Full Name
....

Date & Place of Birth
....

Date & Place of Death

Full Name
....

Date & Place of Birth
....

Date & Place of Death

Full Name
....

Date & Place of Birth
....

Date & Place of Death

Full Name
....

Date & Place of Birth
....

Date & Place of Death

Full Name
....

Date & Place of Birth
....

Date & Place of Death

Full Name
....

Date & Place of Birth
....

Date & Place of Death

Full Name
....

Date & Place of Birth
....

Date & Place of Death

My Great-Great-Grandparents

Full Name
....

Full Name

Full Name
....

Full Name

Full Name
....

Full Name

Full Name
....

Full Name

Full Name
....

Full Name

Full Name
....

Full Name

Full Name
....

Full Name

Full Name
....

Full Name

My Great-Great-Great-Grandparents

Full Name ....   Full Name

Full Name   Full Name

Full Name   Full Name

Full Name   Full Name

Full Name   Full Name

Full Name   Full Name

Full Name   Full Name

Full Name   Full Name

Full Name   Full Name

Full Name   Full Name

Full Name   Full Name

Full Name   Full Name

Full Name   Full Name

Full Name   Full Name

Full Name   Full Name

Full Name   Full Name

My Siblings & Their Families

Fill in all the vital statistics about your siblings and their children.

Name
....

Born
....

Died
....

Partner(s)
....

....

Children
....

....

....

Name
....

Born
....

Died
....

Partner(s)
....

....

Children
....

....

....

Name
....

Born
....

Died
....

Partner(s)
....

....

Children
....

....

....

Name
....

Born
....

Died
....

Partner(s)
....

....

Children
....

....

....

Fill in the names of any legal guardians and/or chosen family members where applicable, including dates, places, and any information you consider appropriate.

....

....

....

....

....

....

....

....

....

....

....

....

....

....

....

....

....

My Siblings & Their Families

Fill in all the vital statistics about your siblings and their children.

Name ....

Born ....

Died ....

Partner(s) ....

....

....

Children ....

....

....

....

Name ....

Born ....

Died ....

Partner(s) ....

....

....

Children ....

....

....

....

Name ....

Born ....

Died ....

Partner(s) ....

....

....

Children ....

....

....

....

Name ....

Born ....

Died ....

Partner(s) ....

....

....

Children ....

....

....

....

Fill in the names of any legal guardians and/or chosen family members where applicable, including dates, places, and any information you consider appropriate.

My Parents' Families

Fill in all the vital statistics about your parents' siblings and their children.

Name ....

Born ....

Died ....

Partner(s) ....

....

....

Children ....

....

....

Name ....

Born ....

Died ....

Partner(s) ....

....

....

Children ....

....

....

Name ....

Born ....

Died ....

Partner(s) ....

....

....

Children ....

....

....

Name ....

Born ....

Died ....

Partner(s) ....

....

....

Children ....

....

....

Fill in the names of any legal guardians and/or chosen family members where applicable, including dates, places, and any information you consider appropriate.

My Parents' Families

Fill in all the vital statistics about your parents' siblings and their children.

Name ....

Born ....

Died ....

Partner(s) ....

....

....

Children ....

....

....

....

Name ....

Born ....

Died ....

Partner(s) ....

....

....

Children ....

....

....

....

Name ....

Born ....

Died ....

Partner(s) ....

....

....

Children ....

....

....

....

Name ....

Born ....

Died ....

Partner(s) ....

....

....

Children ....

....

....

....

Fill in the names of any legal guardians and/or chosen family members where applicable, including dates, places, and any information you consider appropriate.

....

....

....

....

....

....

....

....

....

....

....

....

....

....

....

....

....

My Grandparents' Families

Fill in all the vital statistics about your grandparents' siblings and their children.

Name ....

Born ....

Died ....

Partner(s) ....

....

Children ....

....

....

Name ....

Born ....

Died ....

Partner(s) ....

....

Children ....

....

....

....

Name ....

Born ....

Died ....

Partner(s) ....

....

Children ....

....

....

Name ....

Born ....

Died ....

Partner(s) ....

....

Children ....

....

....

....

Fill in the names of any legal guardians and/or chosen family members where applicable, including dates, places, and any information you consider appropriate.

....

....

....

....

....

....

....

....

....

....

....

....

....

....

....

....

....

....

My Grandparents' Families

Fill in all the vital statistics about your grandparents' siblings and their children.

Name ....

Born ....

Died ....

Partner(s) ....

....

....

Children ....

....

....

....

Name ....

Born ....

Died ....

Partner(s) ....

....

....

Children ....

....

....

....

Name ....

Born ....

Died ....

Partner(s) ....

....

....

Children ....

....

....

....

Name ....

Born ....

Died ....

Partner(s) ....

....

....

Children ....

....

....

....

Fill in the names of any legal guardians and/or chosen family members where applicable, including dates, places, and any information you consider appropriate.

....

....

....

....

....

....

....

....

....

....

....

....

....

....

....

....

....

My Great-Grandparents' Families

Fill in all the vital statistics about your great-grandparents' siblings and their children.

Name ....

Born ....

Died ....

Partner(s) ....

....

....

Children ....

....

....

Name ....

Born ....

Died ....

Partner(s) ....

....

....

Children ....

....

....

....

Name ....

Born ....

Died ....

Partner(s) ....

....

....

Children ....

....

....

Name ....

Born ....

Died ....

Partner(s) ....

....

....

Children ....

....

....

....

Fill in the names of any legal guardians and/or chosen family members where applicable, including dates, places, and any information you consider appropriate.

....

....

....

....

....

....

....

....

....

....

....

....

....

....

....

....

....

....

My Great-Grandparents' Families

Fill in all the vital statistics about your great-grandparents' siblings and their children.

Name ....

Born ....

Died ....

Partner(s) ....

....

....

Children ....

....

....

Name ....

Born ....

Died ....

Partner(s) ....

....

....

Children ....

....

....

Name ....

Born ....

Died ....

Partner(s) ....

....

....

Children ....

....

....

Name ....

Born ....

Died ....

Partner(s) ....

....

....

Children ....

....

....

Fill in the names of any legal guardians and/or chosen family members where applicable, including dates, places, and any information you consider appropriate.

....

....

....

....

....

....

....

....

....

....

....

....

....

....

....

....

....

My Partner's Ancestral Chart

My Partner's Parent's Full Name
....

Date & Place of Birth
....

Date & Place of Commitment
....

Date of Death
....

Place of Burial
....

Occupation(s)
....

....

Their Favorite Things
....

....

My Partner's Full Name
....

Date & Place of Birth
....

Date & Place of Commitment
....

Date of Death
....

Place of Burial
....

Occupation(s)
....

....

....

My Partner's Favorite Things
....

....

....

....

My Partner's Parent's Full Name
....

Date & Place of Birth
....

Date & Place of Commitment
....

Date of Death
....

Place of Burial
....

Occupation(s)
....

....

Their Favorite Things
....

....

My Partner's Grandparent's Full Name

Date & Place of Birth

Date & Place of Commitment

Date of Death

Place of Burial

Occupation(s)

My Partner's Grandparent's Full Name

Date & Place of Birth

Date & Place of Commitment

Date of Death

Place of Burial

Occupation(s)

My Partner's Grandparent's Full Name

Date & Place of Birth

Date & Place of Commitment

Date of Death

Place of Burial

Occupation(s)

My Partner's Grandparent's Full Name

Date & Place of Birth

Date & Place of Commitment

Date of Death

Place of Burial

Occupation(s)

My Partner's Great-Grandparents

Full Name
....
Date & Place of Birth
....
Date & Place of Death

Full Name
....
Date & Place of Birth
....
Date & Place of Death

Full Name
....
Date & Place of Birth
....
Date & Place of Death

Full Name
....
Date & Place of Birth
....
Date & Place of Death

Full Name
....
Date & Place of Birth
....
Date & Place of Death

Full Name
....
Date & Place of Birth
....
Date & Place of Death

Full Name
....
Date & Place of Birth
....
Date & Place of Death

Full Name
....
Date & Place of Birth
....
Date & Place of Death

My Partner's Great-Great-Grandparents

Full Name

Full Name

Full Name

Full Name

Full Name

Full Name

Full Name

Full Name

Full Name

Full Name

Full Name

Full Name

Full Name

Full Name

Full Name

Full Name

My Partner's Great-Great-Great-Grandparents

Full Name ....   Full Name ....
Full Name ....   Full Name ....

Full Name ....   Full Name ....
Full Name ....   Full Name ....

Full Name ....   Full Name ....
Full Name ....   Full Name ....

Full Name ....   Full Name ....
Full Name ....   Full Name ....

Full Name ....   Full Name ....
Full Name ....   Full Name ....

Full Name ....   Full Name ....
Full Name ....   Full Name ....

Full Name ....   Full Name ....
Full Name ....   Full Name ....

Full Name ....   Full Name ....
Full Name ....   Full Name ....

My Partner's Siblings & Their Families

Fill in all the vital statistics about your partner's siblings and their children.

Name
....

Born
....

Died
....

Partner(s)
....

....

Children
....

....

....

Name
....

Born
....

Died
....

Partner(s)
....

....

Children
....

....

....

....

Name
....

Born
....

Died
....

Partner(s)
....

....

Children
....

....

....

Name
....

Born
....

Died
....

Partner(s)
....

....

Children
....

....

....

....

Fill in the names of any legal guardians and/or chosen family members where applicable, including dates, places, and any information you consider appropriate.

My Partner's Siblings & Their Families

Fill in all the vital statistics about your partner's siblings and their children.

Name
....

Born
....

Died
....

Partner(s)
....

....

Children
....

....

....

Name
....

Born
....

Died
....

Partner(s)
....

....

Children
....

....

....

Name
....

Born
....

Died
....

Partner(s)
....

....

Children
....

....

....

Name
....

Born
....

Died
....

Partner(s)
....

....

Children
....

....

....

Fill in the names of any legal guardians and/or chosen family members where applicable, including dates, places, and any information you consider appropriate.

....

....

....

....

....

....

....

....

....

....

....

....

....

....

....

....

....

....

My Partner's Parents' Families

Fill in all the vital statistics about your partner's parents' siblings and their children.

Name ....

Born ....

Died ....

Partner(s) ....

....

....

Children ....

....

....

Name ....

Born ....

Died ....

Partner(s) ....

....

....

Children ....

....

....

....

Name ....

Born ....

Died ....

Partner(s) ....

....

....

Children ....

....

....

Name ....

Born ....

Died ....

Partner(s) ....

....

....

Children ....

....

....

....

Fill in the names of any legal guardians and/or chosen family members where applicable, including dates, places, and any information you consider appropriate.

....

....

....

....

....

....

....

....

....

....

....

....

....

....

....

....

....

....

My Partner's Parents' Families

Fill in all the vital statistics about your partner's parents' siblings and their children.

Name ....

Born ....

Died ....

Partner(s) ....

....

....

Children ....

....

....

Name ....

Born ....

Died ....

Partner(s) ....

....

....

Children ....

....

....

....

Name ....

Born ....

Died ....

Partner(s) ....

....

....

Children ....

....

....

Name ....

Born ....

Died ....

Partner(s) ....

....

....

Children ....

....

....

....

Fill in the names of any legal guardians and/or chosen family members where applicable, including dates, places, and any information you consider appropriate.

....

....

....

....

....

....

....

....

....

....

....

....

....

....

....

....

....

....

My Partner's Grandparents' Families

Fill in all the vital statistics about your partner's grandparents' siblings and their children.

Name
....

Born
....

Died
....

Partner(s)
....

....

Children
....

....

....

Name
....

Born
....

Died
....

Partner(s)
....

....

Children
....

....

....

....

Name
....

Born
....

Died
....

Partner(s)
....

....

Children
....

....

....

Name
....

Born
....

Died
....

Partner(s)
....

....

Children
....

....

....

....

Fill in the names of any legal guardians and/or chosen family members where applicable, including dates, places, and any information you consider appropriate.

....

....

....

....

....

....

....

....

....

....

....

....

....

....

....

....

....

....

My Partner's Grandparents' Families

Fill in all the vital statistics about your partner's grandparents' siblings and their children.

Name
....

Born
....

Died
....

Partner(s)
....

....

Children
....

....

....

Name
....

Born
....

Died
....

Partner(s)
....

....

Children
....

....

....

Name
....

Born
....

Died
....

Partner(s)
....

....

Children
....

....

....

Name
....

Born
....

Died
....

Partner(s)
....

....

Children
....

....

....

Fill in the names of any legal guardians and/or chosen family members where applicable, including dates, places, and any information you consider appropriate.

....

....

....

....

....

....

....

....

....

....

....

....

....

....

....

....

....

My Partner's Great-Grandparents' Families

Fill in all the vital statistics about your partner's great-grandparents' siblings and their children.

Name ....

Born ....

Died ....

Partner(s) ....

....

....

Children ....

....

....

....

Name ....

Born ....

Died ....

Partner(s) ....

....

....

Children ....

....

....

....

Name ....

Born ....

Died ....

Partner(s) ....

....

....

Children ....

....

....

....

Name ....

Born ....

Died ....

Partner(s) ....

....

....

Children ....

....

....

....

Fill in the names of any legal guardians and/or chosen family members where applicable, including dates, places, and any information you consider appropriate.

....

....

....

....

....

....

....

....

....

....

....

....

....

....

....

....

....

....

....

My Partner's Great-Grandparents' Families

Fill in all the vital statistics about your partner's great-grandparents' siblings and their children.

Name ....

Born ....

Died ....

Partner(s) ....

....

....

Children ....

....

....

Name ....

Born ....

Died ....

Partner(s) ....

....

....

Children ....

....

....

Name ....

Born ....

Died ....

Partner(s) ....

....

....

Children ....

....

....

Name ....

Born ....

Died ....

Partner(s) ....

....

....

Children ....

....

....

Fill in the names of any legal guardians and/or chosen family members where applicable, including dates, places, and any information you consider appropriate.

....

....

....

....

....

....

....

....

....

....

....

....

....

....

....

....

....

....

Emigration & Citizenship

Use this space to record the immigration history and citizenship of those who came before you.

Name	Emigrated From/Date	Immigrated To/Date	Became Citizen

Use the following space to record any other information about the places your family came from that you have or can get, as well as the stories of how your ancestors settled where they are now.

....

....

....

....

....

....

....

....

....

....

....

....

....

....

....

....

....

Emigration & Citizenship

Weddings, Partnerships & Commitment Ceremonies

Use this space to record the happy memories around your family unions.

Names	Date/Location	Special Details & Moments

Names	Date/Location	Special Details & Moments

Weddings, Partnerships & Commitment Ceremonies

Names	Date/Location	Special Details & Moments

Names	Date/Location	Special Details & Moments

Religious & Spiritual Occasions

Fill in the details of any religious and/or spiritual celebrations you
and/or your partner have taken part in.

Name
....

Ceremony or occasion
....

Date and location
....

Important participants
....

....

....

Special details & moments
....

....

....

Name
....

Ceremony or occasion
....

Date and location
....

Important participants
....

....

Special details & moments
....

....

....

....

Name
....

Ceremony or occasion
....

Date and location
....

Important participants
....

....

....

Special details & moments
....

....

....

Name
....

Ceremony or occasion
....

Date and location
....

Important participants
....

....

Special details & moments
....

....

....

....

....

Name

....

Ceremony or occasion

....

Date and location

....

Important participants

....

....

Special details & moments

....

....

....

Name

....

Ceremony or occasion

....

Date and location

....

Important participants

....

....

Special details & moments

....

....

....

....

Name

....

Ceremony or occasion

....

Date and location

....

Important participants

....

....

Special details & moments

....

....

....

Name

....

Ceremony or occasion

....

Date and location

....

Important participants

....

....

Special details & moments

....

....

....

Religious & Spiritual Occasions

Name
....

Ceremony or occasion
....

Date and location
....

Important participants
....

....

Special details & moments
....

....

Name
....

Ceremony or occasion
....

Date and location
....

Important participants
....

....

Special details & moments
....

....

....

Name
....

Ceremony or occasion
....

Date and location
....

Important participants
....

....

Special details & moments
....

....

Name
....

Ceremony or occasion
....

Date and location
....

Important participants
....

....

Special details & moments
....

....

....

Places of Worship & of Spiritual Importance

Use the space below to record information about places of spiritual significance to you and your partner, including location, membership, religious affiliation, and any information you consider appropriate.

....

....

....

....

....

....

....

....

....

....

....

....

....

....

....

Our Homes

Fill in the details about the homes you, your partner, and/or your
family members have lived in throughout your lives.

....

Street

....

City

....

State/Province

....

Country

....

Move-in date

....

Move-out date

....

Occupants

....

....

Memorable details

....

....

Street

....

City

....

State/Province

....

Country

....

Move-in date

....

Move-out date

....

Occupants

....

....

Memorable details

....

....

Street

....

City

....

State/Province

....

Country

....

Move-in date

....

Move-out date

....

Occupants

....

....

Memorable details

....

....

Street

....

City

....

State/Province

....

Country

....

Move-in date

....

Move-out date

....

Occupants

....

....

Memorable details

....

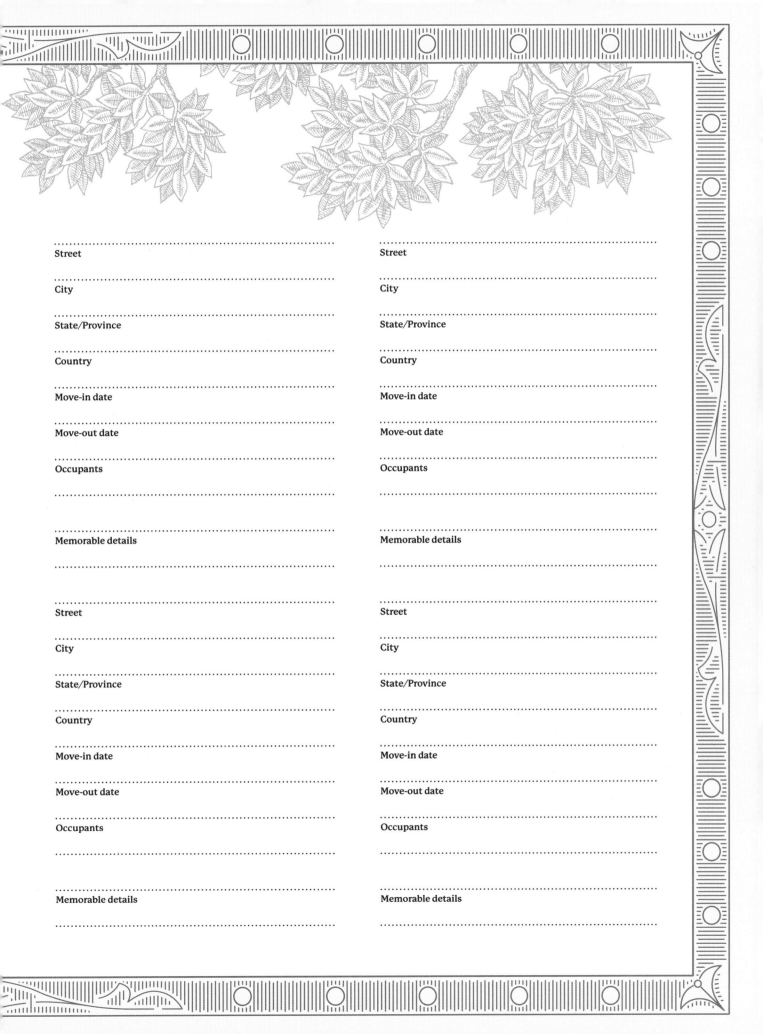

....

Street

....

City

....

State/Province

....

Country

....

Move-in date

....

Move-out date

....

Occupants

....

....

Memorable details

....

....

Street

....

City

....

State/Province

....

Country

....

Move-in date

....

Move-out date

....

Occupants

....

....

Memorable details

....

....

Street

....

City

....

State/Province

....

Country

....

Move-in date

....

Move-out date

....

Occupants

....

....

Memorable details

....

....

Street

....

City

....

State/Province

....

Country

....

Move-in date

....

Move-out date

....

Occupants

....

....

Memorable details

....

Our Homes

....

Street

....

City

....

State/Province

....

Country

....

Move-in date

....

Move-out date

....

Occupants

....

....

Memorable details

....

....

Street

....

City

....

State/Province

....

Country

....

Move-in date

....

Move-out date

....

Occupants

....

....

Memorable details

....

....

Street

....

City

....

State/Province

....

Country

....

Move-in date

....

Move-out date

....

Occupants

....

....

Memorable details

....

....

Street

....

City

....

State/Province

....

Country

....

Move-in date

....

Move-out date

....

Occupants

....

....

Memorable details

....

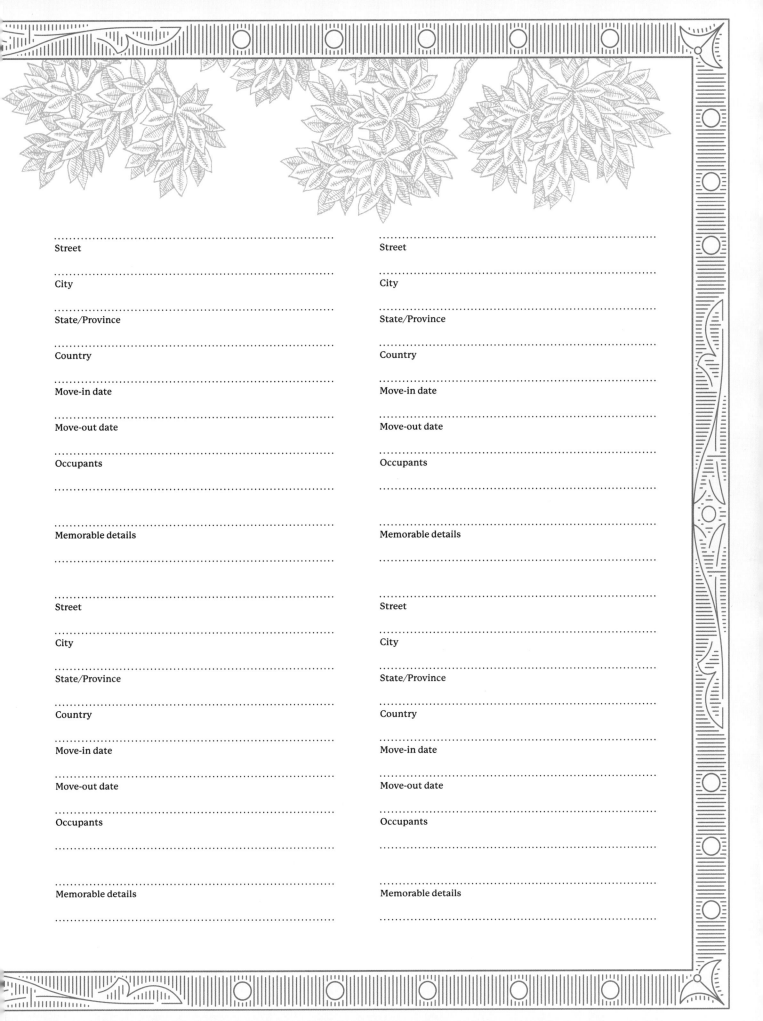

....

Street

....

City

....

State/Province

....

Country

....

Move-in date

....

Move-out date

....

Occupants

....

....

Memorable details

....

....

Street

....

City

....

State/Province

....

Country

....

Move-in date

....

Move-out date

....

Occupants

....

....

Memorable details

....

....

Street

....

City

....

State/Province

....

Country

....

Move-in date

....

Move-out date

....

Occupants

....

....

Memorable details

....

....

Street

....

City

....

State/Province

....

Country

....

Move-in date

....

Move-out date

....

Occupants

....

....

Memorable details

....

Our Ancestral Homes

Trace your and your partner's family homes back through time.
Did generations of your families inherit the same house in the countryside,
or did your homes traverse thousands of miles? Is there a country and culture that
you call home more than a particular house or apartment? Write about all the places
you, your partner, and your families call home.

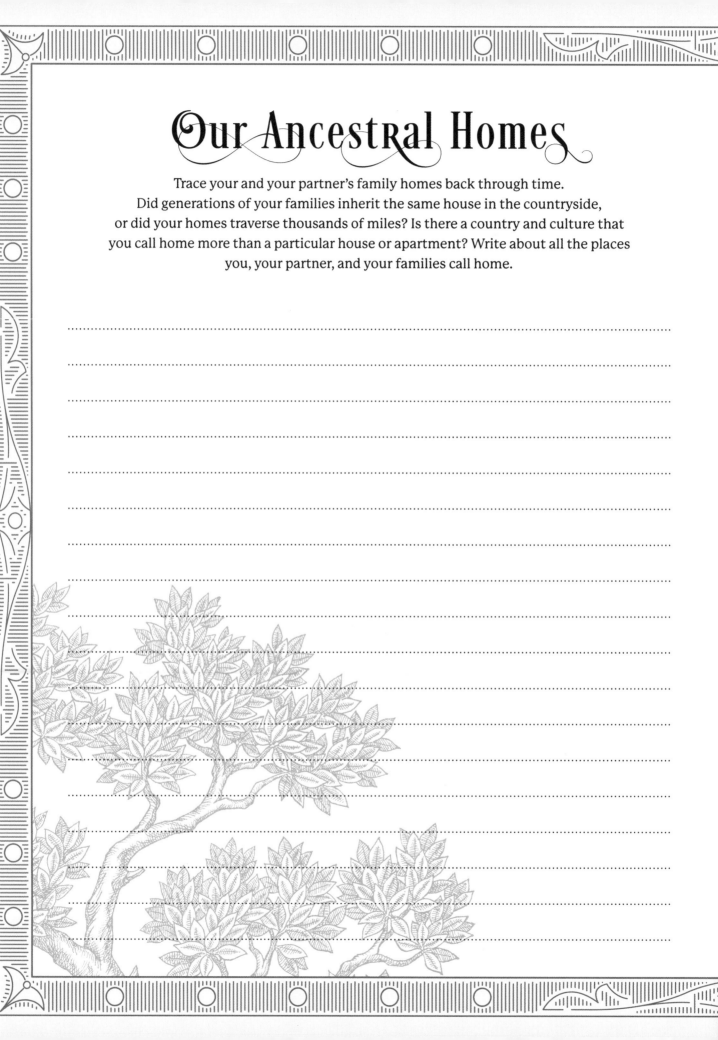

Schools & Graduations

Fill in the information about the schools you, your partner,
and/or your family members attended.

....
Name

....
School, college, or university

....
Dates of attendance

....
Certificate or degree (if applicable)

....

....
Name

....
School, college, or university

....
Dates of attendance

....
Certificate or degree (if applicable)

....

....
Name

....
School, college, or university

....
Dates of attendance

....
Certificate or degree (if applicable)

....

....
Name

....
School, college, or university

....
Dates of attendance

....
Certificate or degree (if applicable)

....

....
Name

....
School, college, or university

....
Dates of attendance

....
Certificate or degree (if applicable)

....

....
Name

....
School, college, or university

....
Dates of attendance

....
Certificate or degree (if applicable)

....

....
Name

....
School, college, or university

....
Dates of attendance

....
Certificate or degree (if applicable)

....

....
Name

....
School, college, or university

....
Dates of attendance

....
Certificate or degree (if applicable)

....

Fill in the details of special friendships or events that occurred during your and your partner's schooling.

....

....

....

....

....

....

....

....

....

....

....

....

....

....

....

....

....

....

....

Notable Achievements

Fill in the details about the milestones you, your partner, and your families have achieved throughout your lives. From learning to swim to getting promoted at work, there are many achievements worth celebrating.

....

Name

....

Achievement

....

Award organization (if applicable)

....

Date

....

....

Name

....

Achievement

....

Award organization (if applicable)

....

Date

....

....

Name

....

Achievement

....

Award organization (if applicable)

....

Date

....

....

Name

....

Achievement

....

Award organization (if applicable)

....

Date

....

....

Name

....

Achievement

....

Award organization (if applicable)

....

Date

....

....

Name

....

Achievement

....

Award organization (if applicable)

....

Date

....

....

Name

....

Achievement

....

Award organization (if applicable)

....

Date

....

....

Name

....

Achievement

....

Award organization (if applicable)

....

Date

....

Fill in the details about the project, event, or mindset shift that led to you, your partner, and your family members achieving these goals.

....

....

....

....

....

....

....

....

....

....

....

....

....

....

....

....

....

....

Clubs & Organizations

Fill in the names of clubs and organizations you, your partner, and/or your family members participated in, whether during your school years or adult life.

....
Name

....
Club or organization

....
Position held

....
Dates

....

....
Name

....
Club or organization

....
Position held

....
Dates

....

....
Name

....
Club or organization

....
Position held

....
Dates

....

....
Name

....
Club or organization

....
Position held

....
Dates

....

....
Name

....
Club or organization

....
Position held

....
Dates

....

....
Name

....
Club or organization

....
Position held

....
Dates

....

....
Name

....
Club or organization

....
Position held

....
Dates

....

....
Name

....
Club or organization

....
Position held

....
Dates

....

Fill in other interesting information about the clubs and organizations, including descriptions of activities, membership responsibilities, and/or events held.

Work History

Record here the employment histories of you, your partner, and your families.

Name ....

Company ....

Industry ....

Dates of employment ....

Position(s) ....

Important milestones and memories

....

Name ....

Company ....

Industry ....

Dates of employment ....

Position(s) ....

Important milestones and memories

....

Name ....

Company ....

Industry ....

Dates of employment ....

Position(s) ....

Important milestones and memories

....

Name ....

Company ....

Industry ....

Dates of employment ....

Position(s) ....

Important milestones and memories

....

Name ....

Company ....

Industry ....

Dates of employment ....

Position(s) ....

Important milestones and memories

....

Name ....

Company ....

Industry ....

Dates of employment ....

Position(s) ....

Important milestones and memories

....

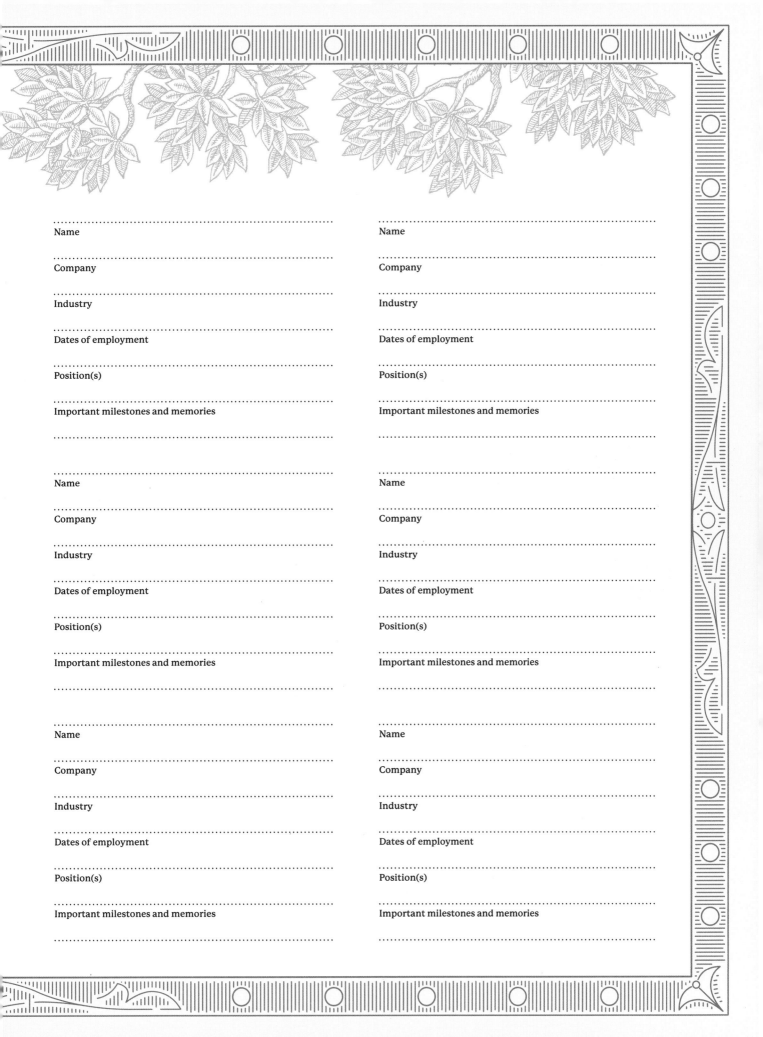

....
Name

....
Company

....
Industry

....
Dates of employment

....
Position(s)

....
Important milestones and memories

....

....
Name

....
Company

....
Industry

....
Dates of employment

....
Position(s)

....
Important milestones and memories

....

....
Name

....
Company

....
Industry

....
Dates of employment

....
Position(s)

....
Important milestones and memories

....

....
Name

....
Company

....
Industry

....
Dates of employment

....
Position(s)

....
Important milestones and memories

....

....
Name

....
Company

....
Industry

....
Dates of employment

....
Position(s)

....
Important milestones and memories

....

....
Name

....
Company

....
Industry

....
Dates of employment

....
Position(s)

....
Important milestones and memories

....

Work History

Name
....

Name
....

Company
....

Company
....

Industry
....

Industry
....

Dates of employment
....

Dates of employment
....

Position(s)
....

Position(s)
....

Important milestones and memories
....

Important milestones and memories
....

Name
....

Name
....

Company
....

Company
....

Industry
....

Industry
....

Dates of employment
....

Dates of employment
....

Position(s)
....

Position(s)
....

Important milestones and memories
....

Important milestones and memories
....

Name
....

Name
....

Company
....

Company
....

Industry
....

Industry
....

Dates of employment
....

Dates of employment
....

Position(s)
....

Position(s)
....

Important milestones and memories
....

Important milestones and memories
....

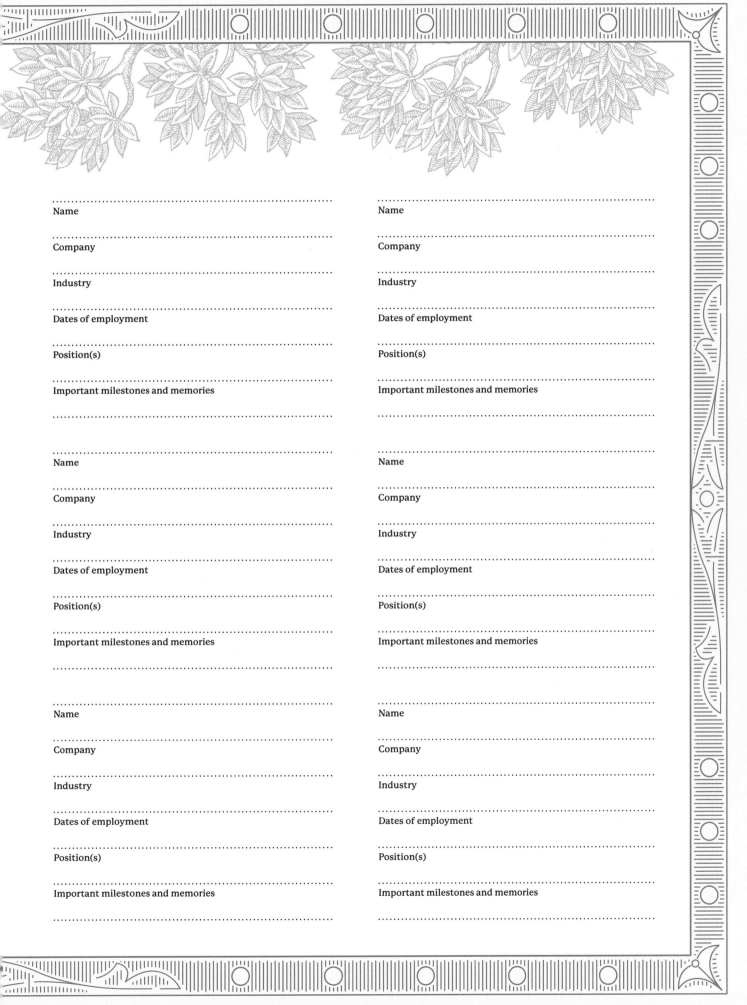

Name

Company

Industry

Dates of employment

Position(s)

Important milestones and memories

Name

Company

Industry

Dates of employment

Position(s)

Important milestones and memories

Name

Company

Industry

Dates of employment

Position(s)

Important milestones and memories

Name

Company

Industry

Dates of employment

Position(s)

Important milestones and memories

Name

Company

Industry

Dates of employment

Position(s)

Important milestones and memories

Name

Company

Industry

Dates of employment

Position(s)

Important milestones and memories

Military & Public Service

Fill in the details of you, your partner, and any members of your families who have held public service positions, including government, police and fire, public works, military, and more.

....
Name

....
Service number (if applicable)

....
Date started

....
Job classification(s)

....
Discharged or date ended

....
Notes

....

....

....

....
Name

....
Service number (if applicable)

....
Date started

....
Job classification(s)

....
Discharged or date ended

....
Notes

....

....

....

....
Name

....
Service number (if applicable)

....
Date started

....
Job classification(s)

....
Discharged or date ended

....
Notes

....

....

....

....
Name

....
Service number (if applicable)

....
Date started

....
Job classification(s)

....
Discharged or date ended

....
Notes

....

....

....

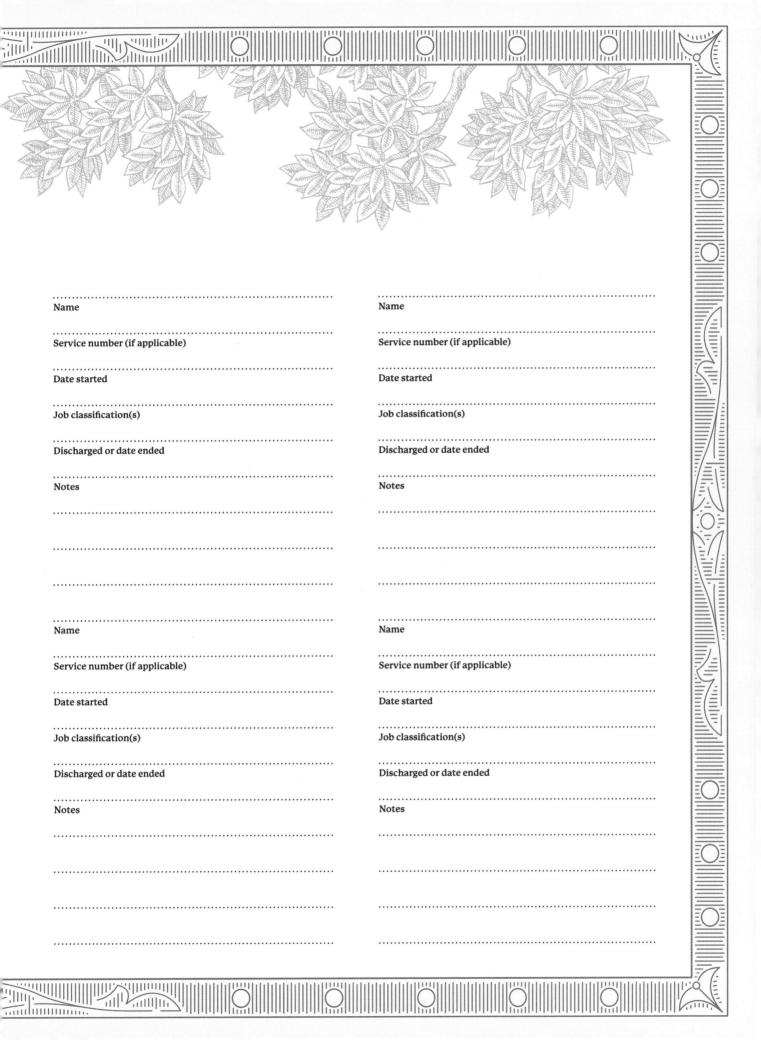

....

Name

....

Service number (if applicable)

....

Date started

....

Job classification(s)

....

Discharged or date ended

....

Notes

....

....

....

....

Name

....

Service number (if applicable)

....

Date started

....

Job classification(s)

....

Discharged or date ended

....

Notes

....

....

....

....

Name

....

Service number (if applicable)

....

Date started

....

Job classification(s)

....

Discharged or date ended

....

Notes

....

....

....

....

Name

....

Service number (if applicable)

....

Date started

....

Job classification(s)

....

Discharged or date ended

....

Notes

....

....

....

....

Military & Public Service

Name
....

Service number (if applicable)
....

Date started
....

Job classification(s)
....

Discharged or date ended
....

Notes
....

....

....

Name
....

Service number (if applicable)
....

Date started
....

Job classification(s)
....

Discharged or date ended
....

Notes
....

....

....

....

Name
....

Service number (if applicable)
....

Date started
....

Job classification(s)
....

Discharged or date ended
....

Notes
....

....

....

Name
....

Service number (if applicable)
....

Date started
....

Job classification(s)
....

Discharged or date ended
....

Notes
....

....

....

....

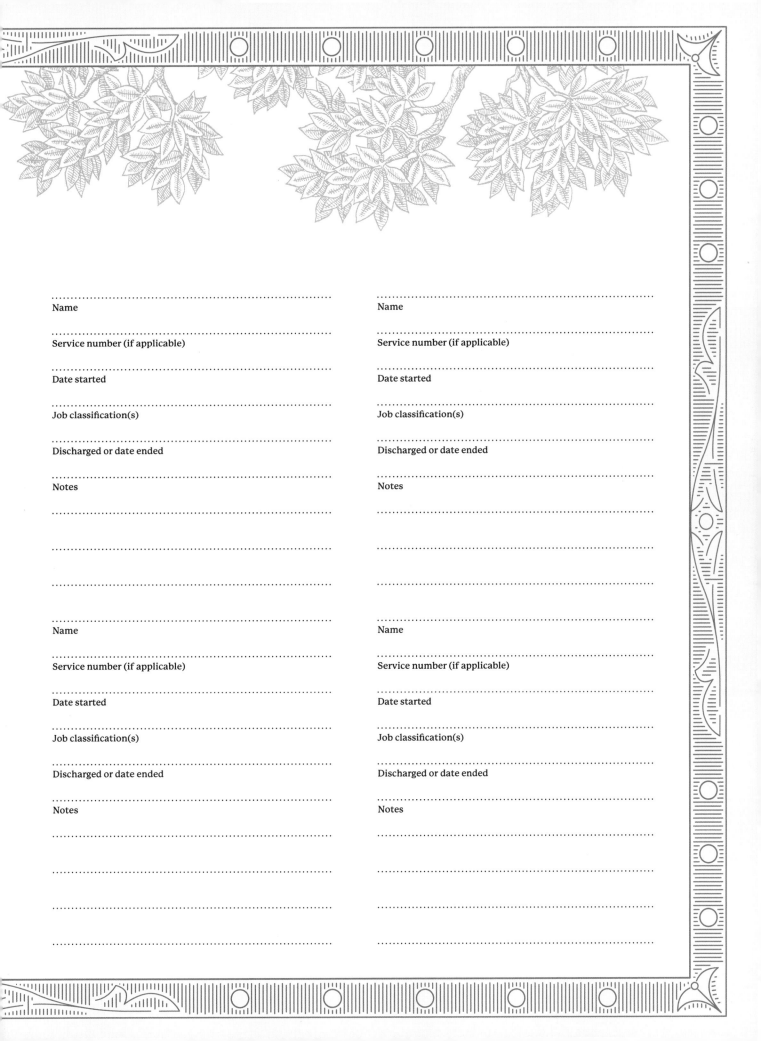

....
Name

....
Service number (if applicable)

....
Date started

....
Job classification(s)

....
Discharged or date ended

....
Notes

....

....

....

....
Name

....
Service number (if applicable)

....
Date started

....
Job classification(s)

....
Discharged or date ended

....
Notes

....

....

....

....
Name

....
Service number (if applicable)

....
Date started

....
Job classification(s)

....
Discharged or date ended

....
Notes

....

....

....

....
Name

....
Service number (if applicable)

....
Date started

....
Job classification(s)

....
Discharged or date ended

....
Notes

....

....

....

Political Affiliations & Important Causes

Fill in the details about any political affiliations or causes that you,
your partner, and your families have participated in.

....
Name

....
Cause/organization

....

....

Date(s) involved

....

....
Name

....
Cause/organization

....

Date(s) involved

....

....
Name

....
Cause/organization

....

....

Date(s) involved

....

....
Name

....
Cause/organization

....

....

Date(s) involved

....

....
Name

....
Cause/organization

....

Date(s) involved

....

....
Name

....
Cause/organization

....

....

Date(s) involved

....

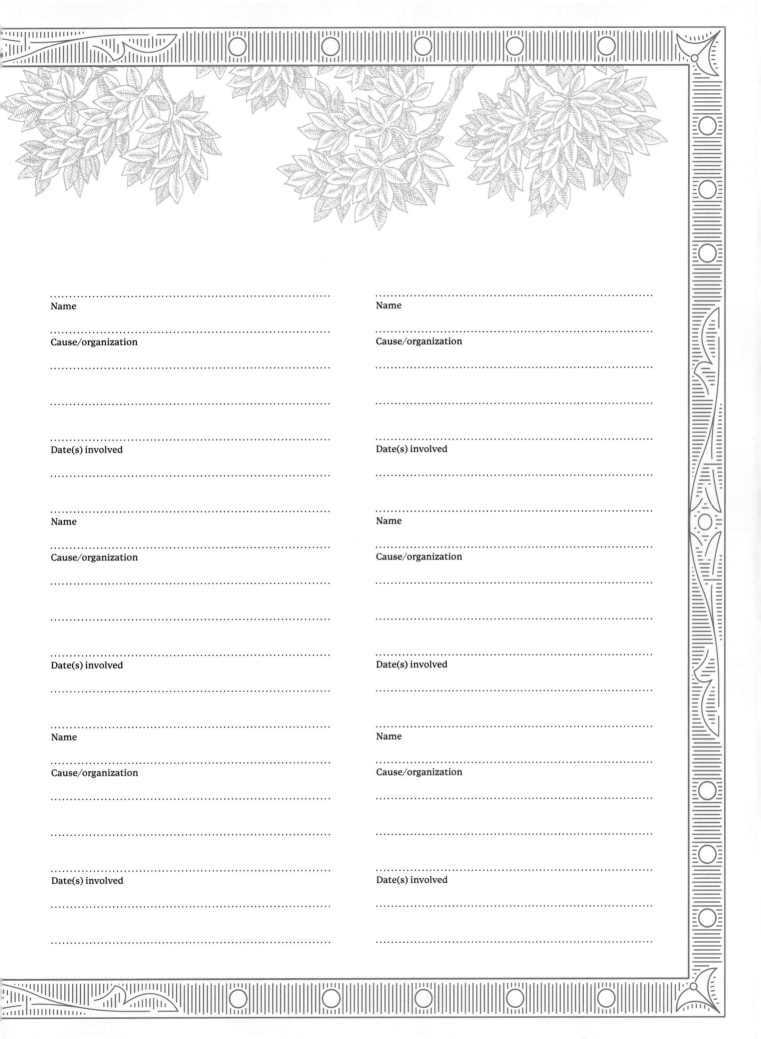

....
Name

....
Cause/organization

....

....

....
Date(s) involved

....

....
Name

....
Cause/organization

....

....

....
Date(s) involved

....

....
Name

....
Cause/organization

....

....

....
Date(s) involved

....

....
Name

....
Cause/organization

....

....

....
Date(s) involved

....

....
Name

....
Cause/organization

....

....

....
Date(s) involved

....

....
Name

....
Cause/organization

....

....

....
Date(s) involved

....

Political Affiliations & Important Causes

Use the space here to elaborate on why you, your partner, and members of your families joined these causes and the memorable events or details that occurred during your membership.

....

....

....

....

....

....

....

....

....

....

....

....

....

....

....

....

....

Our Friends

Ranging from one to many, you and your partner have close friends who
have become family. Write about your and your partner's chosen family, including
when and where you met and the qualities that make them so special to you both.

Our Friends

Our Pets

Like good friends, the animals in our lives become part of the family and one of the most important parts of daily life. Fill in the details about the pets you and/or your partner have helped raise or seen grow up in your families.

....
Owner

....
Pet's name

....
Type of pet

....
Dates of ownership

....
Memorable characteristics

....

....
Owner

....
Pet's name

....
Type of pet

....
Dates of ownership

....
Memorable characteristics

....

....
Owner

....
Pet's name

....
Type of pet

....
Dates of ownership

....
Memorable characteristics

....

....
Owner

....
Pet's name

....
Type of pet

....
Dates of ownership

....
Memorable characteristics

....

....
Owner

....
Pet's name

....
Type of pet

....
Dates of ownership

....
Memorable characteristics

....

....
Owner

....
Pet's name

....
Type of pet

....
Dates of ownership

....
Memorable characteristics

....

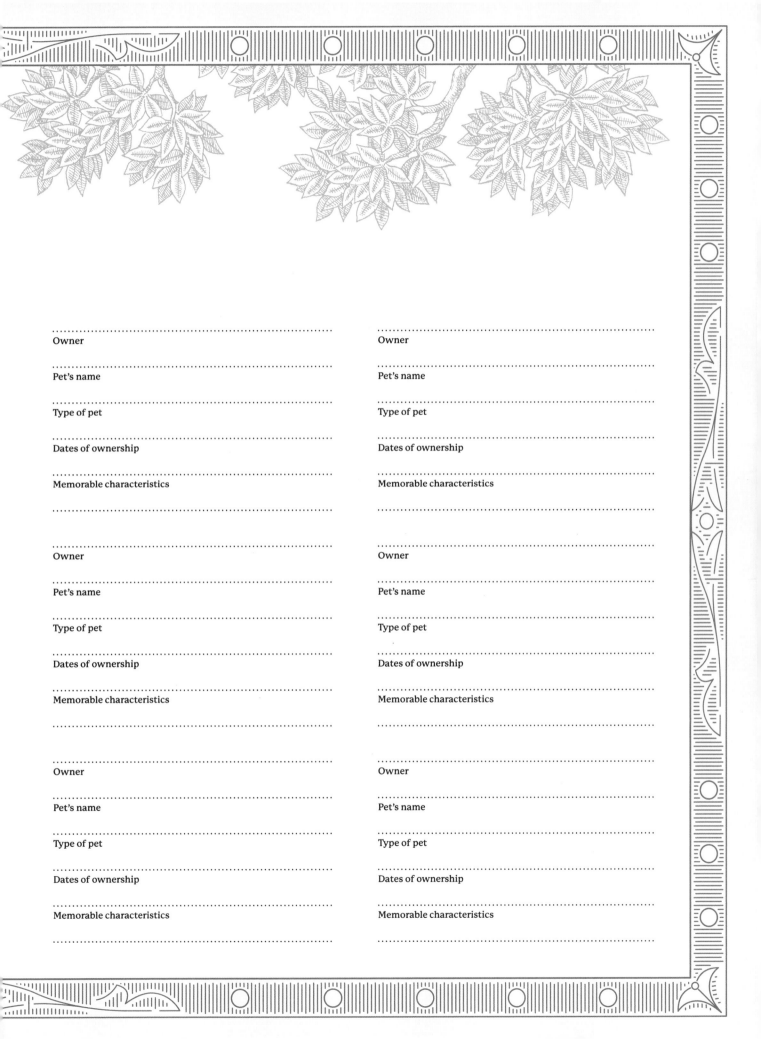

Owner
....

Pet's name
....

Type of pet
....

Dates of ownership
....

Memorable characteristics
....
....

Owner
....

Pet's name
....

Type of pet
....

Dates of ownership
....

Memorable characteristics
....
....

Owner
....

Pet's name
....

Type of pet
....

Dates of ownership
....

Memorable characteristics
....
....

Owner
....

Pet's name
....

Type of pet
....

Dates of ownership
....

Memorable characteristics
....
....

Owner
....

Pet's name
....

Type of pet
....

Dates of ownership
....

Memorable characteristics
....
....

Owner
....

Pet's name
....

Type of pet
....

Dates of ownership
....

Memorable characteristics
....
....

Our Pets

Write down your favorite stories and memories about your pets.

How You Traverse the World

Do you and your partner drive or do you bike everywhere? How much of your getting around involves walking? Fill in the details about your modes of transportation, including current and former ones.

....
Owner/user

....
Type of transportation

....
Make/model (if applicable)

....
Color

....
Dates of ownership/usage

....
Where you went

....

....

....

....
Owner/user

....
Type of transportation

....
Make/model (if applicable)

....
Color

....
Dates of ownership/usage

....
Where you went

....

....

....

....
Owner/user

....
Type of transportation

....
Make/model (if applicable)

....
Color

....
Dates of ownership/usage

....
Where you went

....

....

....

....
Owner/user

....
Type of transportation

....
Make/model (if applicable)

....
Color

....
Dates of ownership/usage

....
Where you went

....

....

....

Use this space to write down any extra details about how you got around (including repairs, trips, memories while on your route) that made an impact on you and your partner.

....

....

....

....

....

....

....

....

....

....

....

....

....

....

....

....

....

....

Our Favorite Things as a Couple

Is it a song, a book, or a recipe? Write about all the things you and
your partner have a shared love for.

....

....

⚬⚭⚬

....

....

⚬⚭⚬

....

....

⚬⚭⚬

....

....

⚬⚭⚬

....

....

⚬⚭⚬

....

....

⚬⚭⚬

....

....

Our Favorite Things with Our Children

From favorite toys to stories, foods to vacation spots, and more, write
about what you and your partner have loved and experienced with your children.

Favorite Sports

Write about your and your partner's favorite sports to either watch or play.
Feel free to include members of your families who played, if applicable.

Name
....

Sport
....

Team/club (if applicable)
....

Achievements (if applicable)
....

Favorite memories
....
....

Name
....

Sport
....

Team/club (if applicable)
....

Achievements (if applicable)
....

Favorite memories
....
....

Name
....

Sport
....

Team/club (if applicable)
....

Achievements (if applicable)
....

Favorite memories
....
....

Name
....

Sport
....

Team/club (if applicable)
....

Achievements (if applicable)
....

Favorite memories
....
....

Name
....

Sport
....

Team/club (if applicable)
....

Achievements (if applicable)
....

Favorite memories
....
....

Name
....

Sport
....

Team/club (if applicable)
....

Achievements (if applicable)
....

Favorite memories
....
....

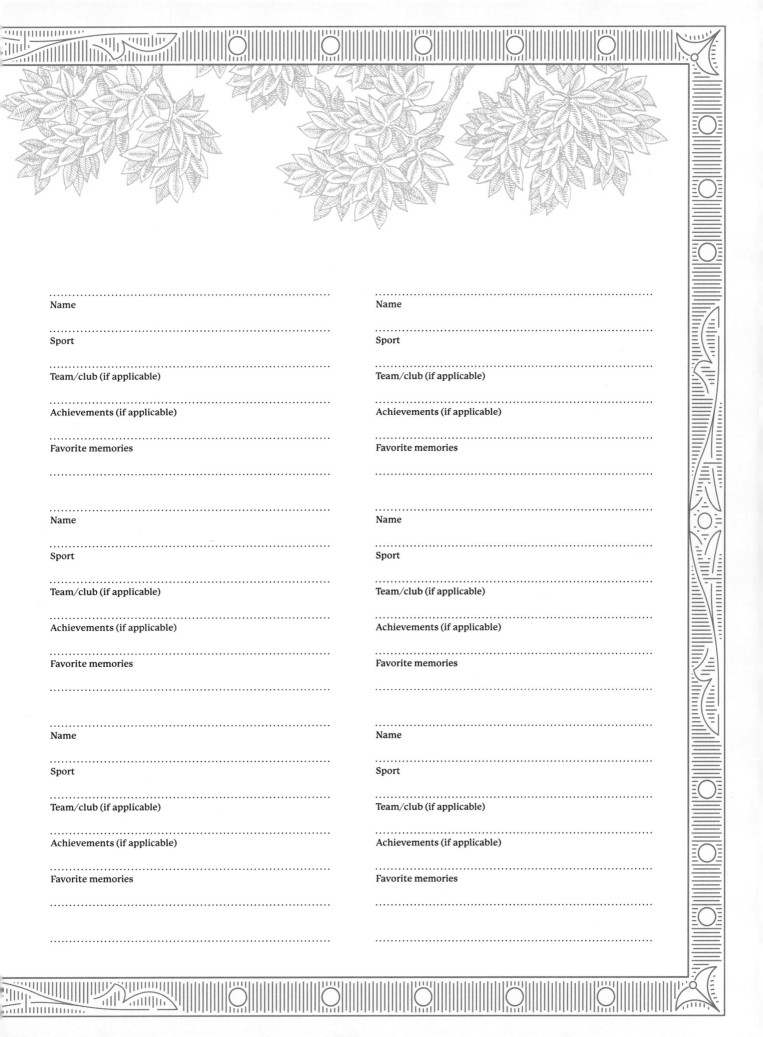

....

Name

....

Sport

....

Team/club (if applicable)

....

Achievements (if applicable)

....

Favorite memories

....

....

Name

....

Sport

....

Team/club (if applicable)

....

Achievements (if applicable)

....

Favorite memories

....

....

Name

....

Sport

....

Team/club (if applicable)

....

Achievements (if applicable)

....

Favorite memories

....

....

....

Name

....

Sport

....

Team/club (if applicable)

....

Achievements (if applicable)

....

Favorite memories

....

....

Name

....

Sport

....

Team/club (if applicable)

....

Achievements (if applicable)

....

Favorite memories

....

....

Name

....

Sport

....

Team/club (if applicable)

....

Achievements (if applicable)

....

Favorite memories

....

....

Favorite Films & Television

Fill in the details of your and your partner's favorite movies and shows.

....
Name

....
Show/movie title

....
Release date

....
Genre

....
Favorite character(s)

....
Favorite scene, episode, or season

....

....
Name

....
Show/movie title

....
Release date

....
Genre

....
Favorite character(s)

....
Favorite scene, episode, or season

....

....
Name

....
Show/movie title

....
Release date

....
Genre

....
Favorite character(s)

....
Favorite scene, episode, or season

....

....
Name

....
Show/movie title

....
Release date

....
Genre

....
Favorite character(s)

....
Favorite scene, episode, or season

....

....
Name

....
Show/movie title

....
Release date

....
Genre

....
Favorite character(s)

....
Favorite scene, episode, or season

....

....
Name

....
Show/movie title

....
Release date

....
Genre

....
Favorite character(s)

....
Favorite scene, episode, or season

....

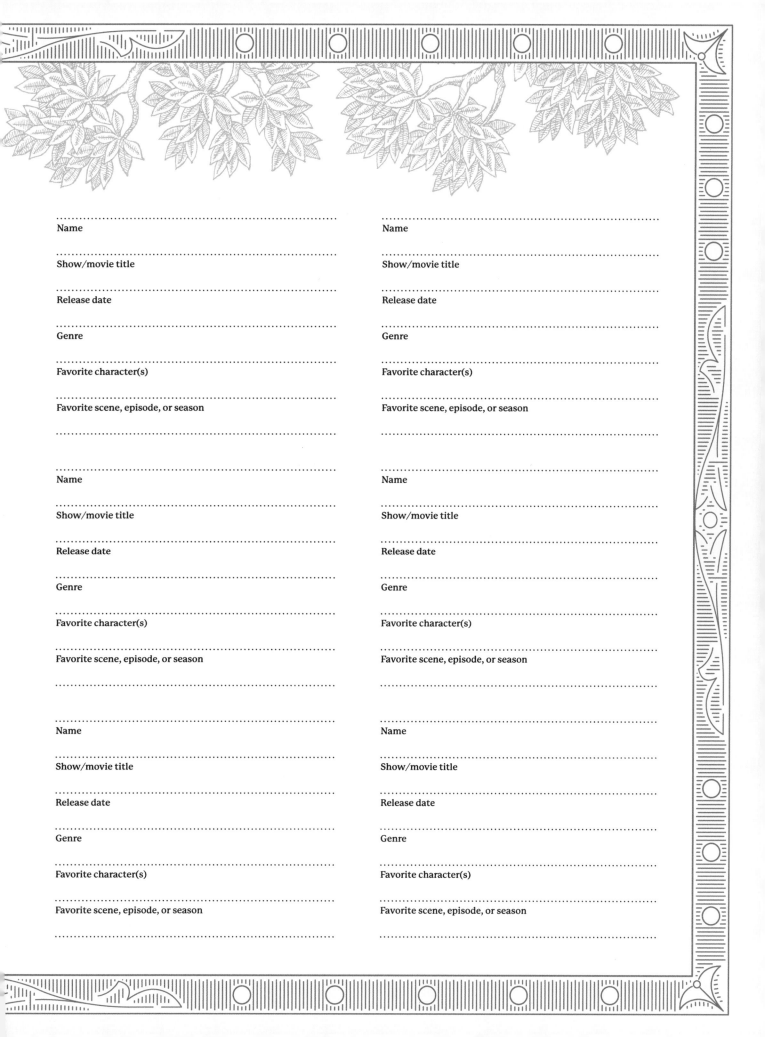

Name

Show/movie title

Release date

Genre

Favorite character(s)

Favorite scene, episode, or season

Name

Show/movie title

Release date

Genre

Favorite character(s)

Favorite scene, episode, or season

Name

Show/movie title

Release date

Genre

Favorite character(s)

Favorite scene, episode, or season

Name

Show/movie title

Release date

Genre

Favorite character(s)

Favorite scene, episode, or season

Name

Show/movie title

Release date

Genre

Favorite character(s)

Favorite scene, episode, or season

Name

Show/movie title

Release date

Genre

Favorite character(s)

Favorite scene, episode, or season

Favorite Books & Other Art

Write about the books and other art forms that have left a big
impression on you and your partner.

....
Name

....
Book/art title

....
Author/artist

....
Favorite aspect/part

....

....

How did it make you feel?

....

....

....

....
Name

....
Book/art title

....
Author/artist

....
Favorite aspect/part

....

....

....
How did it make you feel?

....

....

....
Name

....
Book/art title

....
Author/artist

....
Favorite aspect/part

....

....

How did it make you feel?

....

....

....

....
Name

....
Book/art title

....
Author/artist

....
Favorite aspect/part

....

....

....
How did it make you feel?

....

....

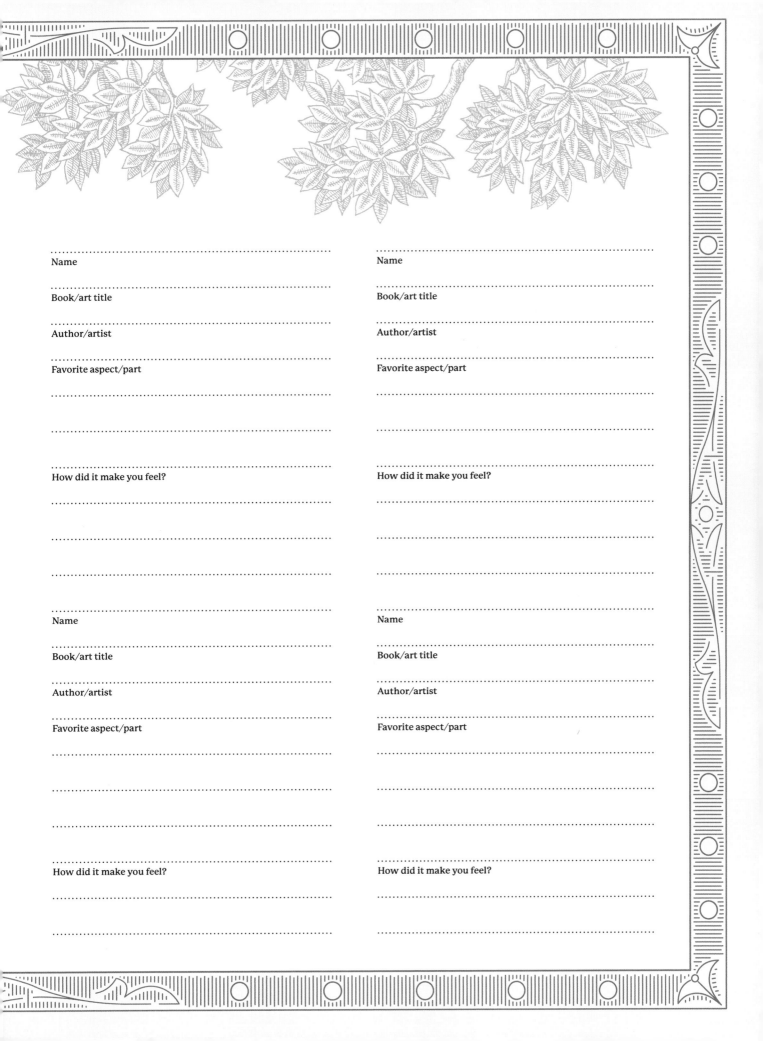

....
Name

....
Book/art title

....
Author/artist

....
Favorite aspect/part

....

....

How did it make you feel?

....

....

....

....
Name

....
Book/art title

....
Author/artist

....
Favorite aspect/part

....

....

....

How did it make you feel?

....

....

....
Name

....
Book/art title

....
Author/artist

....
Favorite aspect/part

....

....

How did it make you feel?

....

....

....

....
Name

....
Book/art title

....
Author/artist

....
Favorite aspect/part

....

....

How did it make you feel?

....

....

Favorite Restaurants & Food Spots

Are you and your partner drawn to restaurants more for their cuisine, the crowd they attract, or the energy they give off? Write about some of your favorite food spots to visit together.

Favorite Music & Live Events

Fill in the details about you and your partner's favorite musical acts, plays, spoken word events, orchestras, operas, and more.

Name

Artist/title

Genre

Favorite song or line

Favorite live event (if applicable)

How did it make you feel?

Name

Artist/title

Genre

Favorite song or line

Favorite live event (if applicable)

How did it make you feel?

Name

Artist/title

Genre

Favorite song or line

Favorite live event (if applicable)

How did it make you feel?

Name

Artist/title

Genre

Favorite song or line

Favorite live event (if applicable)

How did it make you feel?

Name

Artist/title

Genre

Favorite song or line

Favorite live event (if applicable)

How did it make you feel?

Name

Artist/title

Genre

Favorite song or line

Favorite live event (if applicable)

How did it make you feel?

Write more in depth about you and your partner's most memorable music and live events. When did you discover your favorite musician, play, opera, or song? What kinds of memories do you associate with your first viewing or listening experience?

....

....

....

....

....

....

....

....

....

....

....

....

....

....

....

....

....

Favorite Hobbies & Pastimes

Do you and your partner have your own separate hobbies, or do you have some in common?
Write about your favorite ways to pass the time and why you love doing them.

Vacations

Whether to another country or another city, you and your partner (with or without your families) have likely gone away on vacation at some point during your lives. Recall now the places, events, foods, and more that you remember most fondly from these trips. Yes, staycations do count!

Vacations

Reunions

Remembering who was there and at what occasion becomes a lot easier with
a written record. Use this space to recount family reunions big and small, and
the people and events that made them memorable.

....

....

....

....

....

....

....

....

....

....

....

....

....

....

....

....

....

Reunions

Family Traditions

Write about the special traditions passed down through your and
your partner's families over time.

Family Traditions

Collections & Heirlooms

List any special collections and heirlooms that have moved through generations of your and your partner's families, including the original owner (if known) and how the items were passed down.

Collections & Heirlooms

Meaningful Events & Memories

Within all families there are extraordinary events, both good and bad, both planned and unplanned. Use this space to record any memorable experiences within your and your partner's families that you feel are appropriate to write down.

Meaningful Events & Memories

Meaningful Events & Memories

Oral Histories

From survivors to migrants and more, every family has stories that have
never been written down. If comfortable and appropriate, record here
these oral histories to pass them on for generations to come.

Oral Histories

Oral Histories

Illnesses & Hereditary Maladies

Fill in details about illnesses and hereditary maladies
that are present in your families.

....
Name

....
Illness

....
Hospitalization (if applicable)

....
Operation (if applicable)

....
Notes

....

....
Name

....
Illness

....
Hospitalization (if applicable)

....
Operation (if applicable)

....
Notes

....

....
Name

....
Illness

....
Hospitalization (if applicable)

....
Operation (if applicable)

....
Notes

....

....
Name

....
Illness

....
Hospitalization (if applicable)

....
Operation (if applicable)

....
Notes

....

....
Name

....
Illness

....
Hospitalization (if applicable)

....
Operation (if applicable)

....
Notes

....

....
Name

....
Illness

....
Hospitalization (if applicable)

....
Operation (if applicable)

....
Notes

....

Name

Illness

Hospitalization (if applicable)

Operation (if applicable)

Notes

Name

Illness

Hospitalization (if applicable)

Operation (if applicable)

Notes

Name

Illness

Hospitalization (if applicable)

Operation (if applicable)

Notes

Name

Illness

Hospitalization (if applicable)

Operation (if applicable)

Notes

Name

Illness

Hospitalization (if applicable)

Operation (if applicable)

Notes

Name

Illness

Hospitalization (if applicable)

Operation (if applicable)

Notes

Illnesses & Hereditary Maladies

....
Name

....
Illness

....
Hospitalization (if applicable)

....
Operation (if applicable)

....
Notes

....

....
Name

....
Illness

....
Hospitalization (if applicable)

....
Operation (if applicable)

....
Notes

....

....
Name

....
Illness

....
Hospitalization (if applicable)

....
Operation (if applicable)

....
Notes

....

....
Name

....
Illness

....
Hospitalization (if applicable)

....
Operation (if applicable)

....
Notes

....

....
Name

....
Illness

....
Hospitalization (if applicable)

....
Operation (if applicable)

....
Notes

....

....
Name

....
Illness

....
Hospitalization (if applicable)

....
Operation (if applicable)

....
Notes

....

....

Name

....

Illness

....

Hospitalization (if applicable)

....

Operation (if applicable)

....

Notes

....

....

Name

....

Illness

....

Hospitalization (if applicable)

....

Operation (if applicable)

....

Notes

....

....

Name

....

Illness

....

Hospitalization (if applicable)

....

Operation (if applicable)

....

Notes

....

....

Name

....

Illness

....

Hospitalization (if applicable)

....

Operation (if applicable)

....

Notes

....

....

Name

....

Illness

....

Hospitalization (if applicable)

....

Operation (if applicable)

....

Notes

....

Name

....

Illness

....

Hospitalization (if applicable)

....

Operation (if applicable)

....

Notes

In Memoriam

These pages are dedicated to the remembrance of those who have passed on.
Write about your memories, the things that those you've lost loved, and
any other pertinent information about them.

In Memoriam

Photographs & Keepsakes

Attach favorite clippings, mementos, documents, and photos from
your and your partner's families.

Photographs & Keepsakes

10 9 8 7 6 5 4 3 2 1

ISBN: 978-1-57715-373-3

Publisher: Rage Kindelsperger
Creative Director: Laura Drew
Managing Editor: Cara Donaldson
Editor: Sara Bonacum
Editorial Assistant: Zoe Briscoe
Cover Design: Beth Middleworth
Interior Design: Ashley Prine, Tandem Books

Printed in China